Lost Stories
of
South Africa

BOOK ONE

Published by
LifeTime Creations

www.lifetimecreations.com

In this issue

The war that went badly wrong

EXTRACT FROM: *Sent to Kill* by Graham Fysh, the complete story of the war against King Moorosi in 1879.

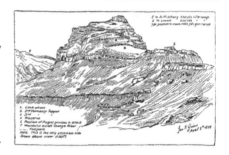

Hopes for victory are high when, shortly after dawn, Griffith calls the army of Cape Mounted Riflemen together on the grassy parade ground at the foot of Moorosi's mountain in what is today Lesotho.

He outlines his plan of attack. "We estimate Chief Moorosi to have 200 to 300 followers with him on the mountaintop," Griffith says. "The mountain, as you can see, is inaccessible on three sides. We are calling the face behind me, the only accessible part, the 'attacking side.' It is steep and consists of a succession of three ledges, or tiers, one above the other. The Baphuthi have made excellent use of these natural ledges by building flanking walls on them.As you have no doubt observed, Moorosi's men are well armed and some are positioned behind the ledges.

"At sunrise tomorrow, around 6 o'clock, we will start pounding the mountain with the seven-pounder guns. Once these formidable weapons have subdued the enemy and opened a way for us to attack, the men in the cave under Grant will rush forward on to the plateau, to be shortly followed by those troops on this side. I suspect that most of the rebels will flee ahead of you. Your march to the top should be relatively easy.

"When you reach the top, you will take prisoner all who surrender and you will find and arrest Moorosi. I see no reason we should not be able to accomplish these tasks in one day. We could even be having breakfast with Moorosi tomorrow."

That failed to happen. To find out how the war went wrong and what happened next read *Sent to Kill*, available in online bookstores.

WEATHER

THE SOUTHEASTER, which blows strongly during the Cape Town summer months, once was called the *Cape Doctor* by a humorist because it blew the filth of the city into the sea.

The name stuck and some people still call it that today.

Here's support for that nickname: In 1857 *The Cape Argus* complained of a calm February. "The protracted absence of the Cape Doctor or Scavenger-General and the unseasonable weather—an unprecedented amount of rain—have seriously affected the public health. The result is measles, scarlatina, diphtheria, with a retinue of complaints described as seediness, all-overishness and sinking."

It's been worse

Those who say every year that the south-easter is "stronger than ever" might consider this note by Lawrence Green in *Tavern of the Seas* in 1927:

The south-easter squalls tear across the Cape Flats with hurricane force...A roof in the suburbs has gone with a rumbling, grating sound. Telephone lines are down and orchards are being stripped of their fruit. Plate glass windows are shattered by the sudden pressure. A mountain fire is roaring down on the houses at Camps Bay, fragments of pine bark burning like rockets in the wind.

Anything above 75 miles an hour ranks officially as a hurricane. The southeaster exceeds that mark every summer. Gusts often have reached 102 miles an hour.

BY THE WAY: The prevailing wind in the summer comes mainly from the south, not the south-east. But the name south-easter has stuck and it seems pointless now to try to rename it.

The Great East Coast Storm of 1874

Widespread disastrous floods ravaged the east coast of South Africa in December 1874.

A report of the event published at the time said: "Rain fell not in drops, but in sheets, which caused every river and every stream to overflow its banks and rush down to the sea with terrible force.

"Such bridges as were not high above the water were washed away; many houses were wholly or partly destroyed; cultivated ground disappeared, leaving only bare rock or barren subsoil and great numbers of sheep and horned cattle were drowned." In East London five vessels were wrecked and the at Port Natal two vessels were wrecked.

The Doorn River flood of 1875

In December 1875, the Doorn River, which runs through the village of Heidelberg in the Cape, suddenly flooded. "It carried away 45 houses with all their contents, with the loss of two lives," a contemporary report reads. "The gardens along the course of the stream were completely destroyed, all the soil being washed away."

A peculiarity of this storm was that the flood cut a deep channel along a line, whereas not a rain drop fell a few hundred paces on each side of it.

I CAN SAFELY SAY that even the air of Wynberg on the one side, and of Green and Sea Points on the other side of Cape Town, are very good atmospheres for invalids, and indeed far better than can be found at most times of the year at any so-called sanitaria in the United Kingdom or the continent of Europe.

— *Dr. Harry Leach (Medical Officer for the Port of London), 1880*

The story behind a

MOUNTAINOUS SCAM

It was around 1697 when a man arrived at the doorstep of the new Groot Constantia mansion into which old man Simon van der Stel had moved six years earlier when he became governor.

Simon van der Stel

At the time Van der Stel, head of the Dutch East India Company in the Cape Colony, already had done pretty well for himself in terms of prestige and wealth. Now he was being presented with another chance to make money.

After getting past the guards, the crafty character reached Simon and held in his hands a mass of silver. "Look at this, he told the unsuspecting governor. Pure, unadulterated silver. It is merely a sample of what I found not far from here. There's lots more where this came from."

Van der Stel, ever interested in making big money quickly, was impressed. Coins and fine objects around the world were made of silver. Here was a potential fortune to be

Groot Constantia

made, not just for him but also for the colony, which could do with a good boost of income.

"Where did you get this from?" Van der Stel asked.

"It's from a rich mine that I found on Simonsberg", the man replied. "As you know, the mountain is named after you. Now your mountain will reap a fine return on that name."

Then followed the catch. "I need money to work the mine. A substantial amount of money. Just put me in control and I will work it myself. It should not be long before I will deliver the first batches of silver to the company. And there will be plenty more where this came from.

Simonsberg

"In the meantime you can keep this chunk of silver for yourself."

The next day Van der Stel traveled to government headquarters in the Castle in Cape Town for a meeting with the Policy Council. He showed them the silver.

Then he persuaded them to advance a substantial amount of money to the man to work the mine. After all, to mine the silver he would need spades, pick axes, oxen and wagons for transporting the precious metal. Oh yes, and he would have to employ people to help him.

Key chain

He also ordered the mass of silver that the man had given him to be made into a chain to which the keys of the Castle gates should be attached. It would be a memento of the first piece of silver that started the colony on the road to riches.

The chain was made. But the huge haul of silver never materialized.

The man disappeared.

An embarrassed Van der Stel launched an investigation into the silver claims. The investigators took a short while to find that the silver had come from a number of Spanish dollars that had been melted down.

No signs of even a small silver mine on Simonsberg were found. Not only that. The Dutch East India Company's coffers were short a substantial amount of cash that had been forwarded to the con man.

For years afterward the chain continued to hold the Castle gate keys as "a memorial of the credulity of the governor and the council," according to author John Barrow who picked up the story when he traveled to the colony and the interior of South Africa in 1797 and 1798.

WEIRD EVENTS

Two gunshots lay between
feast and famine

B ack in 1754 every ship that put into Table Bay was required to fire a salute of nine gunshots, upon which the Castle would reply with seven. When a French ship arrived in March 1754 to anchor in Table Bay, her captain refused to salute unless the fortress, out of respect, would return an equal number of nine shots. Apparently that was a big deal in those days.

The governor was unavailable, but the secunde (deputy), a man named Swellengrebel, informed the French captain, who had come on shore, that no provisions would be supplied until he conformed to the usual custom of seven gunshots. He could get water and firewood, but nothing more.

The Frenchman returned to his vessel, but failed to fire a single shot. "You agree to fire nine shots in return," he said, "or we do not fire. Even if we starve." He would wait out in the bay until the Cape governor would see the error of his ways and agree to fire nine shots in reply.

A month later, in April, another French ship sailed into Table Bay. The captain also demanded nine shots in return or nothing. No, said Governor Ryk Tulbagh back in charge once more. He would not allow even a single supply boat to travel out to either of the ships.

At length one of the French captains offered to fire the required number of guns for both vessels. The governor replied that each ship must fire; one could not fire the guns on behalf of the other.

The captains held out a little longer, but at length submitted. Each of the French ships fired their promised nine shots. The Castle replied with only seven shots. The French accepted that. They came on land and their crews were treated in a most friendly way and supplied with whatever provisions they needed. Why the original refusal? Go figure.

WHEN
CHILD NAMES
BECAME A PROBLEM

BY THE TIME Miles Bowker and Ann Maria Mitford, who lived in Albany in the Eastern Cape, had their seventh child in 1812, they had run out of names. They had used all the traditional names in calling their first six sons John, William, Miles, Thomas, Bertram and Robert.

In desperation they named their seventh son Septimus, the Latin name for seven. He was followed by another boy. What the heck, they figured. They called him Octavius, the Latin name for eight.

Child number nine was—at last—a girl. They named her Mary Elizabeth. She was followed by Anna Maria. Conventional names at the time for girls.

When the eleventh child was born, he turned out to be another boy. But calling him the Latin for eleven – undecimus – did not sound right. If nothing else, it would be negative in nature. They resorted to James Henry. Just as well. There was nothing un... about him.

James Henry Bowker became commandant of the Frontier Armed and Mounted Police and later High Commissioner of Basutoland (today's Lesotho). Bowker Street in Escombe, Durban, is named after him.

He never married. He probably did not know what he would name his children if he did.

The Bowker

Boys

SEPTIMUS   OCTAVIUS   JAMES HENRY

The Ovambo people who live in what is today's Namibia had their own form of gun control hundreds of years before guns were invented. During the season when the marula tree yielded a strong form of wine, Ovambo leaders ruled that no man could carry a knife, spear or club.

FORGOTTEN SCANDAL

Priest DESTROYED by community he helped

A MONG THE first scandals to hit the newly established town of Knysna in the 1850s involved an Anglican minister and an unpaid loan.

The 38-year-old Dr. Andrews, who arrived from England in 1849 to take the ministerial position, had a heavy load to carry. And by all accounts he carried it well; perhaps too well. Consider:

* He had charge over a large parish, 50 miles in extent, from Swart River in the west to Keurbooms River in the east, which he was expected to cover by horseback and on foot;
* His parishioners expected him to be both a medical as well as a spiritual doctor;
* He helped build the original St. George's Church in Knysna; and

The church Dr. Andrews helped to build is on the right in this 1885 photograph.

* From his stipend of £100 a year (R100 000 today) he had to pay for a home for his family in addition to a stable stocked with a horse, forage, harness and a groom.

"He was at the beck and call of every nuptial ceremony, every child birth, every baptism, every sick-bed, every death-bed, every graveside and every other human drama peculiar to village life", records Winifred Tapson in *Timber and Tides: The story of Knysna and Plettenberg Bay*, published in 1963. "He was like a will-'o-the-wisp, appearing here, there and everywhere in all manner of guises. Now at Belvidere, helping T.H. Duthie with the building of his little St. George's Church; now at Plettenberg Bay holding service in W.H. Newdigate's little church in the Pisang Valley, or in Melville with his parishioners on Sundays in a licensed place of worship. On weekdays he taught the village children in their little school, presided at church meetings, and invited churchwardens and sidesmen to dinner to meet the Bishop on his visitations."

After three years of serving the spiritual needs of the Knysna community, Dr. Andrews sought financial help to build a house. He struck a deal with a Captain Horn. Dr. Andrews would pay for the labour and Horn for the material. At the end of nine months the loan would be repaid with money Dr. Andrews expected from an inheritance in England.

The legacy failed to materialise, however, and Dr. Andrews was unable to pay back the loan. The longer he delayed in paying the loan, the more his financial problems grew, but he refused to rescue himself by charging for his medical services. He was too caring for his flock.

Efforts by Bishop Robert Gray to raise a fund for the priest were only marginally successful. Neither generosity nor forgiveness were among the attributes of the wealthier citizens of Knysna at that time.

Dr. Andrew's wife died in 1855, leaving him with seven young children. He was devastated. By 1858 his health had deteriorated so much that the priest asked for leave and returned to England.

He left just in time, Tapson recalls. Nine leading churchmen signed a document refusing to have Dr. Andrews back. The bishop was pressured into appointing a commission of inquiry, which found his "sinful" failure to pay back the loan outweighed all the good he had done for the community's physical and spiritual health.

Dr. Andrews resigned with effect from June 30, 1860. He died on November 8, 1864 in Grosvenor Square, London. He was 53.

FEATURE STORY

How South Africa battled

250 YEARS

of

PANDEMICS

Whereupon smallpox broke out in the Cape Colony in February, 1713, the then ruling Dutch East India Company authorities wondered how the virus had reached the colony's shores.

They knew it must almost certainly have been introduced from outside the colony. That much was clear.

They knew, too, that almost all the new entrants to the colony came from passengers and crew on sailing ships that arrived regularly in Table Bay.

When they consulted the list of recent arrivals, however, they found that recent passengers were not responsible for transmitting the virus. The people who had contracted the virus had had no contact with them. As they investigated further they found that the most likely origin was not person-to-person. The virus, they concluded, had been transmitted in another way.

It turned out that the clothes of an infected crew member of a ship in the harbour had been washed in a river near the Castle. The drinking water became contaminated and the disease spread through the community in that way.

> Smallpox is a highly contagious, disfiguring and often deadly disease caused by the variola virus. It killed some 300 million people worldwide in the 20th Century before becoming the only human infectious disease ever to be completely eradicated.

The virus spread quickly and before long the epidemic was severe. Hospitals became crowded and the death rate was high.

At one stage so many died that the authorities ran out of wood for coffins.

Those who contracted the disease were isolated.

In time the rate of transmission slowed and within a few months the epidemic was over. Life returned to normal. So much so that for the following 42 years the dreaded disease was absent from the Cape Colony. The residents thought they had defeated it in 1713 and believed they would never see it again.

Virus returns

Then in 1755, it came back. With a vengeance. Again from abroad.

At first the settlers did not believe the fever was smallpox. But after a few days they had no doubt. The original flu-like symptoms were followed by a rash on the face, hands and forearms and later on the rest of the body.

As before, the Dutch East India Company authorities searched out the source of the new scourge. They knew that again it had to be from outside the colony.

Their questions on how the disease had reached their shores were soon answered. A ship returning home to Europe from Ceylon had stopped at the Cape in late April to stock up on produce. Sailors, happy to be on land again, at least for a while, walked up the streets of Cape Town. They were welcomed. They were fed. They mingled with the people.

These greetings were a regular occurrence. After all, the Cape had been established as a refreshment station about 100 years before. Feeding sailors and supplying their ships with produce for export was a major part of the life of the town. It was a major reason the settlement existed.

But the people of the Cape Colony did not know at the time that a smallpox pandemic was sweeping the world. They found out only later after extensive inquiries that sailors had brought the killer disease with them and the pandemic had reached their shores.

They knew, too, that there was no cure for smallpox. Patients could only be made comfortable as the disease ran its course, resulting in a high death rate.

Table Bay 1752
From an original painting in the Fairbridge Collection

By June an increasing number of people had become infected with the deadly disease.

The Cape colony residents realised that this time the outbreak was far more severe than it had been in 1713.

It was so contagious that almost everyone in Table Valley (later called Cape Town) contracted it. And it was so deadly that it seemed everyone who contracted it died from it.

Family member infected family member. Neighbour infected neighbour. The colonists were unsure who was spreading it and how it was spreading. They had no idea how to stop it.

So many sick people filled the hospitals that the nurses and doctors could not cope.

To handle the surge in cases, the Dutch East India Company, which ran the colony at that time, built two large hospitals. One was for the poor people of European extraction; the other was for the black people, many of them slaves. The cost of caring for the slaves was borne by the slave owners who were required to pay a shilling and 4 pence a day for each slave (about R300 today).

In addition to the hospitals, the cemeteries became full. The burial ground around the church in Cape Town was filled up. Another had to be opened. For that purpose, on June 21 the Council of Policy of the

Dutch East India Company granted 42 hectares adjoining the military burial ground between Lion's Rump (later Signal Hill) and the shore of Table Bay.

Colony could be wiped out

As autumn turned to winter, the weather became colder than usual. Aided by the cold wet conditions, the disease stepped up its virulent offensive.

During the calendar month of July alone 1,102 people in the small community died.

The disease was an equal-opportunity killer. Of those who died in July, 489 were of European extraction, 33 were free blacks and 580 were slaves. Slaves outnumbered Europeans at the time.

Cemetries became full

Some recovered from the disease. Those who did were hired as nurses as they were then immune.

The Dutch East India Company authorities realised that if the disease continued to ravage the community at the same rate and remained unchecked, Table Valley would be wiped out.

But they had no idea how to stop its rapid advance.

Sharp drop in values

As it swept through the community in Table Valley, the pandemic wrecked the economy. The value of property fell so sharply that the sale of houses ground to a halt. The main sources of personal wealth, such as jewellery, silver plates and silver cutlery, were impossible to sell to raise money. Business ground to a halt.

The fees charged for graves in the newly established cemeteries were similar to those in the existing ones, but many families of smallpox victims were not charged because of the dire state of their personal finances.

Church services were poorly attended. The government excused the militia from having to muster for drill.

In the country areas, people remained on their farms to avoid coming into contact with the disease. Little produce was taken by wagon for sale to the Cape for several months.

As a result, the town of Stellenbosch, 50 km from Table Valley, was spared, according to the memoirs of Petrus Borcherds, who served as Civil Commissioner and resident magistrate of Cape Town. His book was published in 1861.

"Owing to preventative measures it did not reach Stellenbosch," he writes. Those measures were presumably isolation. Nevertheless the disease spread inland to other areas, exacting a heavy toll on the Khoikhoi who suffered considerably more than they had in 1713.

It is not possible to say how far it extended, but its ravages were felt in Great Namaqualand at least for the 26th parallel of latitude and in the east to the Bashee River, writes historian George Theal in *The History of South Africa under the Administration of the Dutch East India Company* (published in 1897).

Heavy toll on Khoikhoi

As the weather warmed and spring arrived, the disease slowed its pace, but nevertheless from May 1 to October 31, 2,071 people died (963 Europeans and 1,109 blacks) from smallpox.

That number was a major portion of the people who lived in Table Valley and about a quarter of the then total population of the colony. They had died in just six months.

"If that death rate had continued, before the close of the year there would have been no one remaining," Theal writes.

Relief finally arrived in Table Valley when the weather became warmer. The disease became less virulent and fewer people were infected. The hot weather and the sun as well as people spending more time outdoors helped to eradicate it. Before midsummer it died out entirely.

But that was not to be the end of the Cape's experiences with smallpox.

Disease reappears

In 1767 a Danish ship returning to Europe from India again brought smallpox to the Cape Colony. It was prevalent in Cape Town from May until November, but the people had learned from experience to avoid close contact with one another and this time the disease took less of a toll and was less deadly.

It remained a killer, however. A total of 1,800 to 1,900 people caught the disease. Of those, 583 (179 Europeans, 145 free blacks and 259 slaves) died.

Although the hot weather had caused the disease to die out in 1713 and 1755, this time it was not until April 1769, two years after it began, that it completely disappeared.

The hot weather in summer, however, played a significant role in reducing the number of deaths and eventually in eliminating the smallpox outbreak before autumn and cooler weather arrived.

Smallpox re-appeared in the colony in 1807 when on June 16 a prisoner in Cape Town was found to be suffering from it. He had recently arrived from Algoa Bay, today's Gqeberha (Port Elizabeth).

The sick man and two prisoners with whom he had been in contact were taken to Rentzkies Farm, a thatched farmhouse in Paarden Island, close to Milnerton.

There, they were kept in strict isolation. All three recovered. Owing to the precautions taken, the disease did not spread and no other case was discovered, Theal records.

Five years later smallpox was again to rear its head in the Cape.

The epidemic of 1812

On March 15, 1812 almost 100 years after the first smallpox epidemic hit the Cape, a slave from a condemned Portuguese ship was found to be suffering from the disease, although he had appeared to be well when he first landed.

He was at once isolated, but soon other cases were discovered in the community and the disease spread rapidly.

Fear spread through the community.

A vaccination against smallpox had been developed by Edward Jenner in 1796 and was coming into widespread use around the world. The Cape Colony government issued instructions that everyone in town should be inoculated, but many Muslims refused to do so on religious grounds. Others were also suspicious of the new treatment, believing that it might harm them rather than protect them.

The previous outbreak had made it clear that the disease spread easily from person to person. As a result, steps were taken to curb people gathering together to keep the disease from spreading too far and too fast among those who were not inoculated.

Schools and churches closed

Schools and places of worship were closed. Businesses were ordered to shut their doors and people were told to avoid communicating with others at a close distance.

When the disease appeared in a house, a white flag was hung outside and those coming from such a house were required to wear strips of white calico around their arms.

This time the precautions were more effective than 70 years previously. A combination of the vaccine and the isolation resulted in only a few hundred cases occurring.

In addition, the strain of smallpox seemed to be milder than before.

As a result, most of those who fell victim to the disease recovered.

Those living in the country areas refused to visit Cape Town. Communications with the interior almost stopped.

But, according to Petrus Borcherds's memoirs, the disease did reach Stellenbosch this time.

An Early Example of

Contact Testing and Tracing

This notice was included in the report of John Woodhead, the Mayor of Cape Town in his report for the year ending September 27, 1894.

Notification of Infectious Diseases

Under this heading I am glad to be able to record that a most progressive and wise step has been taken by the Council.

About the beginning of last year (Mayoral year) a request was made to the local Practitioners of Medicine that they should voluntarily notify each week the Infectious Diseases coming under their notice. This appeal was most heartily responded to by the Doctors and this voluntary notification continued to the middle of March, 1894. By the help of this system the Sanitary Superintendent was able to do much useful work in remedying causes of disease.

In March, 1894, I had the honour to suggest to the Sanitary Committee that they should bring Section 176 of the Cape Town Municipal Act, 1893, under the notice of the Medical Practitioners of the Town, and thus practically establish the Compulsory Notification of Infectious Diseases.

My report was adopted, and since that date the compulsory system of notification of Infectious Diseases, such as is in vogue in the larger towns in Great Britain, has been in full swing within your Municipality.

Since its establishment the system has worked most smoothly and satisfactorily, and by its means the Medical Officer is able to keep his finger on the weak sanitary spots through the agency of the Sanitary Superintendent and his staff of Inspectors.

A practical illustration of its value was afforded in the case of the recent outbreak of Smallpox. The case was at once reported and thus dealt with before further harm was done.

No epidemic can be sprung upon the Municipality now without the Health Authority being immediately aware of it, and all precautions taken to prevent its spread and investigate its origin.

Cape Town, as is only right, has in this matter led the van of Sanitary Science in the Colony, and has every reason to be most proud of its achievement.

"The vaccine, which by the prudent arrangement of government had been introduced by Dr. White of the 83rd regiment, checked the calamity," he writes.

"I had the satisfaction of seeing that —from out of the arms of my second daughter then about four years old whom I held on my lap during the operation (the vaccination)—not less than one hundred and eighty individuals were vaccinated."

Isolation and vaccination measures worked

In Cape Town, the warmer weather combined with the vaccinations helped eradicate the disease. By September the disease entirely disappeared and the 11th of October was observed as a day of thanksgiving to God for its cessation.

New measures developed

Experience in dealing with smallpox over the years and an understanding of how it was transmitted later led to measures that effectively controlled outbreaks of the disease.

An outbreak of smallpox in Cape Town in 1882 was described at the time as severe, but vaccinations and isolation measures kept it from becoming as bad as outbreaks in earlier years.

A new development was that those who caught the disease were isolated in a newly developed hospital for contagious diseases at Rentzkies Farm. Here, the newly invented telephone, which had just been introduced in Cape Town, enabled patients to talk with their family and friends without exposing them to the risk of being infected.

The Medical Officer of Health at the time, Dr. G.H.B. Fisk was later commended for his services in coping with the outbreak of the disease at the time.

Transvaal outbreak

In 1893 an "alarming" outbreak of smallpox occurred in the Transvaal. The authorities acted quickly to stop it spreading to the Cape.

"The serious spread of the disease in the Transvaal has had the effect of drawing the attention of all local authorities and responsible bodies throughout the colony to the necessity for the adoption of the best known and most reliable precautionary measures in order to guard against an extension of this loathsome disease," the mayor, John Woodhead, recorded in his annual notes.

He pointed to special powers in new laws that would enable the Sanitary Department to "more effectively trace cases of disease should they occur and thus ensure that no time should be lost in dealing with the same."

Discovered in time

A case of smallpox that occurred at the Table Mountain Reservoir Works on June 9, 1893 was happily discovered in time to prevent any spread of the infection; and the prompt means which were immediately taken to isolate the patient and his companions were successful in confining the outbreak to the case in question.

"Since the appearance of the disease in the City every effort has been made to induce general vaccination, and the readiness with which your appeal to the public has been met in this connection induces the belief that any serious epidemic need not be feared."

In 1894 a new infectious disease hospital was built alongside the New Somerset Hospital in Green Point.

Later all children in South Africa were vaccinated against smallpox and it was eventually eradicated throughout the world in 1977.

THE KATIA PEOPLE, believed to be among South Africa's oldest indigenous people, lived in the semi-desert regions of the Kalahari. They hardly knew what water was. There were few rivers or streams in the area. They depended on wild melons to quench their thirst. The water in the melons would have been uncontaminated and they contained many vitamins and minerals.

The Katia also ate bulbs and roots. The men's average height was 1.5 metres.

They wore no clothes.

LOST TREASURE

RARE DIAMONDS
found in
ABANDONED DIGGINGS

Sketch by J. Vavione, 1881

Are there more still to be found?

O f all the mining camps that sprang up on the quiet banks of the Vaal River during the great rush in the first year of the discovery of diamonds in South Africa, that of Gong-gong, or "laughing waters," was undoubtedly the most picturesque, wrote A.B. Ellis in *South African Sketches* in 1887.

1887

"The diggings near Barkly West attracted hundreds of prospecting   parties who were scattered up and down the river. A few trial holes were dug, and, the yield of diamonds being good, work was commenced in earnest, diggers flocked in, and the camp was established," Ellis wrote.

Gong-gong falls

"Gong-gong, however, never attained great pre-eminence as a camp, and though some 200 claims were opened, they were soon abandoned for the superior attractions of nearby Cawood's Hope and Seven Hells and later the dry diggings at Du Toit's Pan and the New Rush (later named Kimberley).

"In December, 1871, only a score of tents stood dotted about among the clumps of acacia, which still fringed the confusion of the yawning pits and unshapely heaps of stones of the disused claims. In time Gong-gong became the Sleepy Hollow of the Diamond Fields and was all but forgotten," Ellis wrote.

But later, after the diggings had been abandoned and after Ellis had written his article, rare distinctive diamonds were found there. Clearly the diggers had not searched thoroughly enough as shown by subsequent discoveries.

Examples:

* In 1907 a 121 carat diamond was found. It was named Otto Bergstroom.

* In 1916 a 192 carat diamond found at Gong-gong. It was named Dan Campbell.

* In 1921 a 381-carat diamond was named The Arc. The year 1924 recorded two finds of 135 carat and 110 carat diamonds, both unnamed.

* It was here, too, that a superb example of a diamond with silver hue was found in the 1930s. The highly rare specimen weighed in at 153 carats. According to author Lawrence Green, it was sold for £3,200 at the time, which would be about R3.5 million today.

* Are more large and rare diamonds to be found at Gong-gong? Has the site really been dug out? Probably, but can anyone be sure?

FROM The Bank of Leather: one of many fake bank notes in circulation in the 1880s on the Diamond Fields around Kimberley. —*Incwadi Yami* by J.W. Matthews (1887)

PAST PICTURES

Can you identify where and about when these pictures were taken?

Answers: Page 64

NAME ORIGINS

Explorer left his mark on place names

GORDON'S BAY on False Bay near Cape Town was named after Robert Jacob Gordon who explored and mapped large areas of the Western Cape from 1777 to 1780. Gordon, who was Dutch but whose family was of Scottish descent, served as commander of the garrison for the Dutch East India Company from 1780 to 1795 when the British forces first took control of the Cape from the Dutch.

It is not clear why the bay was named after Gordon because he originally named it De Combuis (the kitchen) on the first of his travels.

Also named after him were **Gordon's Kop** in the Sneeuberg and **Gordon's River**, which feeds into the Plettenberg River, but this name does not appear to be in use any longer.

On one of his expeditions into the interior, Gordon named the **Orange River** after Prince William of Orange who appointed him to his post at the Cape and was the then ruler of the Netherlands. Gordon admired the prince and felt a personal allegiance to him.

PRESS SNIPPETS

Opened in 1912, the Alhambra Picture Palace was Cape Town's leading cinema for many years. It had a sliding roof which rolled open on hot nights.

Money went further 100 years ago

MONEY was worth more a century ago. A four-roomed cottage in Cape Town with water laid on was advertised in The Argus for £2 15s. a month.

One may appreciate the extent of the wealth of the richest man at the Cape, Jonas van der Poel, whose wealth on his death in December, 1857, was stated by The Argus to be anything from £300,000 to £600,000. The money was left to six heirs, of whom several bore the name of Hiddingh.

But if money went a longer way, human life was shorter a century ago. The death notices in The Argus show a heavy mortality among children, and though accidents were few it was common for people to die in the twenties and thirties. Old age was the exception.

SERVANT problems were not unknown in 1857, and there was keen competition in securing the services of some 80 immigrants who arrived from St. Helena in March. They were chiefly domestic servants but included skilled tradesmen, gardeners, tailors and carpenters.

'Very high wages' were consequently offered for female servants, reported The Argus. The high wages were £1 15s. a month.

1957

Both clippings are from The Cape Argus.

The reference to "100 years ago" in the article alongside is to 1857.

Money was denominated in pounds (£), shillings (s) and pence (d). In 1961 a pound became worth R2.

OLD TIME COOKING

The kitchen at the Drostdy Museum in Swellendam, Western Cape gives an idea of the utensils used for cooking in the 1800s.

When
CAPE COOKING
was an art

T he art of cooking was an essential element in every home in the Cape Colony from the time it was founded. Today, we have all but lost that art. Fast food, prepared meals and microwaves combined with active working lives that have no time for cooking have taken its place.

Those who still enjoy cooking at home, however, might want to replicate cooking methods and recipes from that time, particularly those traditional dishes that were and still are uniquely South African.

Here is an extract from the introduction to a recipe book prepared by the doyen of South African cooking at that time, Hildagonda Duckitt.

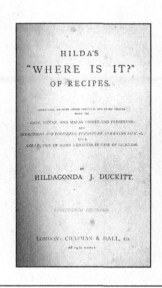

The book, *Hilda's 'Where is it' of Recipes*, was first published in 1891. Even at the time, Hildagonda Duckitt commented, "Few colonial cooks of the present day understand the art of cooking; it is therefore absolutely necessary for the lady of the house to know something about it, so that she can direct them." This extract sheds light on the cooking methods used and the way in which meals were prepared as long as 150 years ago.

SIMMERING (to bring as near as possible to boiling without letting it boil) is one of the great difficulties. Cooks will not remember how much depends on slow cooking.

Hashes, curries, "breedees" etc., etc., must simmer. Fry the onion with the meat, a light brown ("smoor" as Cape cooks say). This must be done rather quickly; then the meat must simmer with whatever ingredient you like to add.

The old Cape families of Dutch descent, who had Malay and Indian cooks, and many of French descent, understood the art of ROASTING. They roast their chickens, partridges, quail, wild duck, venison, etc., not in an oven, but in a flat, round pot, about five and a half inches deep (Dutch baking-pot), with a raised lid.

The meat is put into the pot with, say, half a pint of water, and the pot is put on the stove. About half an hour afterwards some live coals are put on the lid, and just before the joint or chicken begins to brown it is basted well with a little butter or dripping. Half an hour before serving, the cook should pour half a tumbler of red wine, well mixed with a small dessert-spoonful of flour, over the joint or chicken, while giving the gravy a good stir. This gives a delicious flavour to any poultry or venison. A leg of Mutton done in a Dutch baking-pot in this way is very good.

In **BOILING** meat, a leg of mutton, or chicken, etc., be very careful that the water boils when you put it in, and then let it simmer. The meat will be tender and juicy—this is my experience.

Boil all green vegetables—viz., peas, cabbage, green beans, etc.—in an open saucepan; put them into boiling water, into which a teaspoonful of salt and a pinch of carbonate of soda has been added. This is the American mode of cooking vegetables. The peas, beans, etc, will be beautifully green and delicate.

BROILING is the most primitive way of cooking, and it best understood by our country folk. It is, nevertheless, one of the most appetising ways of cooking a mutton chop; and any one who has travelled in South Africa will remember how good was the "Sasatie" (kabob) or tender "carbonatje" (mutton chop), steaming hot from the gridiron on wood coals, or two-pronged fork held against the coals.

Some kinds of fish broiled are very good, such as the Cape "harder," "Hottentot fish" or "snoek."

STEWING is a very easy and economical way of cooking. First stew the meat and onions together, with a very little water, till nice and tender and slightly brown; then add cauliflower, green beans, potatoes, or any vegetable you like. This should be done in a flat pot, not a deep saucepan. Meat and vegetables done in this way are called by the Malay cook a "breedee." Add a red chilli cut small, or a few pieces of it.

In **FRYING** fish, cutlets, etc., be very careful that the lard or clarified dripping in which you do it is boiling. Do not forget to dust your fish with flour, and dip it into an egg-and-bread-crumb mixture, before putting it into the frying-pan.

The tail of the native Cape sheep—which is composed entirely of fat, and often weighs five or six pounds—when minced and melted out, supplies the Cape housewife with a very good substitute for lard; is excellent for frying fish or fritters in; it is more delicate than lard, and eaten on hot toast, with pepper and salt, is a good imitation of marrow.

Always dry any pieces of stale white bread you have, cutting off the crust; pound in a mortar, and keep in a tin closed up, ready for dusting rissoles or cutlets before frying.

PRESERVES—In making marmalades and jams always oil the preserving-pan with the best Lucca Oil, to prevent the jam from burning. If dry sugar is used for preserving, keep the pot closed till the sugar is dissolved, stirring occasionally. When the sugar is melted, jams should boil briskly. In preserving fruit, such as figs, citrons, etc., boil very slowly—simmer, in fact.

Great care should be taken to keep all kitchen utensils scrupulously clean. Washing soda will thoroughly cleanse and remove any taste or smell adhering to saucepans or cans in which onions or cabbage have been cooked. One ounce of washing soda and a gallon of boiling water will go a long way.

Brooke's (Monkey brand) Soap is most excellent for scouring the inside of enamelled saucepans, and for brightening coppers and all tin things used in a kitchen. It also cleans marble washstands, mirrors, window-panes, etc. In cleaning dishes and plates, be careful first to wipe out all greasiness with a piece of paper, and then wash with blue mottled soap in very warm water, and rinse off in clean hot water, and dry and brighten with a nice clean cloth.

OLD CAPE RECIPE

TOMATO BREEDEE

Cape. Hildegonda Duckitt

Cut up two pounds of ribs of mutton and an onion; let it stew in a flat pot for an hour.

Cut up and add eight or ten tomatoes in slices, also a teaspoonful of salt, a pinch of sugar, and half a red chilli.

If there is a great deal of liquid, remove the lid, and let it simmer till it is all a rich, creamy-looking sauce.

Remove the fat. Serve with plain boiled rice.

A very nice entree.

KHOIKHOI: 'Happiest people on earth'

Portrait of the famous Khoikhoi chief Jan Jonker Afrikaner, in European dress.
(From a photograph in the South African Public Library)

When Jan van Riebeeck arrived in what is today Cape Town he and his crew came across local people who called themselves Khoikhoi, or men of men. They had lived in the Cape for possibly thousands of years.

Here s a look at some of the aspects of Khoikhoi life at that time, gathered from writings more than 100 years ago.

No serious illnesses

"Probably, if intellectual enjoyment be excluded, the Hottentots (Khoikhoi) were among the happiest people in existence," historian George McCall Theal recorded in his 1918 book, *Ethnography and Condition of South Africa Before 1505*.

"They generally lived until old age without serious illness. They did not allow possible future troubles to disturb them, and a sufficiency of food was all that was needed to make them as merry and light-hearted as children at play."

Theal adds that "a more improvident, unstable, thoughtless people never existed."

"Those who had cattle were without care or grief, he says, and usually spent the greater part of the day sleeping.

"They delighted, however, in dancing by moonlight to music, which they produced from reeds similar to those used by the Bushmen (San), but superior in tone and effect.

Hospitality was unbounded

"Visitors of rank were also welcomed and entertained with dancing and music.

"Their hospitality to peaceable strangers as well as to individuals of their own clan was unbounded."

The Khoikhoi clans were named after the chiefs who led them. They added "qua" (meaning people of) to the names of the chiefs, hence the Namaqua were the people at one time led by Nama. Other names were the Gonaqua and the Griqua.

Believed in God

The Namaqua, in common with other Khoikhoi, believed in a supreme being. They called him Tsiu-Goab, or Heisi-eibib, recorded Dr. Theophilus Hahn, a missionary's son who lived among the Namaqua and learned to speak their language. Tsiu-Goab was a powerful and beneficent being, who lived in the red sky.

Jan Jonker's wife
(From a photograph in the South African Public Library)

The first missionaries used the word Tsiu-Goab to signify God.

The Khoikhoi also believed in a devil.

A powerful evil being, named Gaunab, lived in the black sky and harmed men, who on that account feared and worshipped him, Hahn added.

Family ties were strong. Near relatives, such as father and daughter, showed strong affection.

The highest oath a man could take, and still takes, was to swear by his eldest sister, Theal records. A man can never address his own sister personally; he must speak to another person to address the sister in his name, or in the absence of anybody he says so that his sister can hear, I wish that somebody will tell my sister that I wish to have a drink of milk.

The eldest sister can even inflict punishment on a grown-up brother if he omits the established traditional rules of courtesy and the codes of etiquette.

Aged and helpless left to die

They abandoned aged and helpless people, even their own parents, as well as sickly and deformed children, whom they usually left in some lonely place and allowed to die of hunger, Theal records.

But they regarded this as mercy, not as cruelty, Theal says. They believed it was better that the sufferers themselves should give up life at once than linger on in misery. If they gave birth to twins, if they were of different sexes the female was thrown away. If they were of the same sex the weaker of the two met that fate.

They were polygamous in some cases. A wealthy man was allowed to take a second wife when his first wife became old or infirm, but he was required to see to the maintenance of the first wife.

Incest was totally forbidden.

GAME OF STONES

A SIMPLE GAME involving small stones was played by the Khoikhoi of South Africa hundreds of years ago:

Two or more people sat on the ground. Each had a small pebble concealed in a folded hand. One player threw both arms out against his opponent, at the same time calling out that he met or that he evaded. His opponent threw his arms out in the same way, so that his right hand was opposite the first player's left, and his left opposite the first player's right. The clenched hands were then opened. If the pebbles were found to be in the same hands, the first player won if he had called out that he met, or lost if he had called out that he evaded. Young men and boys often spent whole nights in this amusement.

Khoikhoi undertook a long...
Journey from Somalia

The Khoikhoi people are believed to have originally hailed from Somalia, and arrived at the southern tip of Africa after traveling for hundreds or even thousands of years down the African continent until they landed up at the southernmost tip of the continent.

Five main reasons are given for this belief:

Language

Parts of speech in the original Khoikhoi language were almost identical to those in **Old Egyptian**. Two students of language came to the same conclusion independently. One was Dr. James Adamson, the first minister of the Presbyterian Church in Cape Town and a professor of mathematics at the South African College.

He reported to the Syro-Egyptian Society that "the signs of gender were almost identical in the Namaqua and the Egyptian languages, and the affix (added to the root of a word) might be considered the same in the Namaqua, Galla (a language spoken in eastern Africa), and Old Egyptian."

In the 1860s Dr W.H.I. Bleek linked the Khoikhoi language to **Hebrew**—an indication that the Khoikhoi people originally came from the Middle East. The composition in Khoikhoi poetry seems to be same as that for the Semitic poets, he wrote in *Comparative Grammar of South African Languages*. "The parallelism which in the Psalms and other poetical portions of the Old Testament takes the place of the rhyme, meter and alliteration of the Aryan languages seems also to constitute the essential quality of Khoikhoi poetry."

Tradition

Missionaries and others who spent many years among the Korana clans found that the Khoikhoi traditions spoke of a period when they lived in a region somewhere in the centre of the continent from which they were driven by a more powerful people.

Animals

The Khoikhoi owned horned cattle and sheep covered with hair and having large tails that are similar to Syrian sheep.

Drilled stones

Strange shaped stones were found in Somalia that are highly similar to those used by the Khoikhoi in South Africa.

The Queen of Punt

A relief showing the queen of Punt (likely Somalia) on a visit in about 1500 B.C. to Egypt is considered by some scholars to be a caricature, or showing a person suffering from a disease, but South Africans have seen it as a portrait of the people who eventually left eastern Africa and settled in what is today the Cape Province.

A theory is that the Khoikhoi moved down the African continent under pressure from stronger people who forced them to move south.

When they reached the central part of the continent, they would have come across the tsetse fly that would have been fatal to their animals. To avoid the tsetse fly they turned westward to the shore of the Atlantic Ocean before turning again to the south.

In southern Africa they came across the San people, who lived in most of the whole of today's South Africa. As herders, the Khoikhoi prided themselves upon their superiority over the San hunters, says George Theal in his *History of South Africa before 1505.*

The Queen of Punt
—from an Egyptian relief

Khoikhoi hut
—from a drawing by William J. Burchell

Although the two peoples were unfriendly toward one another, some Khoikhoi men, who outnumbered the Khoikhoi women, are believed to have married San women.

A Khoikhoi story:

The Dove and the Heron

THE JACKAL, it is said, came once to the dove who lived on the top of a rock and said, "Give me one of your little children." The dove answered, "I shall not do anything of the kind." The Jackal said, "Give it to me at once, otherwise I shall fly up to you." Then she threw one down to him.

He came back another day and demanded another little child, and she gave it to him.

After the jackal had gone, the heron came, and asked, "Dove, why do you cry?" The dove answered him, "The jackal has taken away my little children; it is for this that I cry." He asked her, "In what manner can he take them?" She answered him, "When he asked me I refused him; but when he said, I shall at once fly up, therefore give it to me, I threw it down to him."

The heron said, "Are you such a fool as to give your children to the jackal who cannot fly?" Then, with the admonition to give no more, he went away.

The jackal came again and said, "Dove, give me a little child." The dove refused and told him that the heron had told her that he could not fly. The jackal said, "I shall catch him."

So, when the heron came to the bank of the water, the jackal asked him: "Brother heron when the wind comes from this side, how will you stand? He turned his neck toward him and said, "I stand thus, bending my neck on one side."

The jackal asked him again, "When a storm comes, and when it rains, how do you stand?" He said to him, "I stand thus, indeed, bending my neck down." Then the jackal beat him on his neck and broke his neck in the middle.

Since that day the heron's neck is bent.

—This story was collected by the Rev. Mr. Kronlein in Namaqualand and translated by Dr. Bleek in 1864.

> Klaas Velletjes, a Khoikhoi man from the Kenhardt district, was taken to London in the 1880s where he met Queen Victoria and the royal family. When he returned to work as a shepherd in South Africa he wore a bowler hat and morning coat bearing the labels: "Made expressly for H.R.H. the Prince of Wales."

THUMBTALE

Modimolle

Are we there yet?

The town of Nylstroom (Nile Stream) in Limpopo Province was so named because the white farmers who trekked north and settled there in the 1860s thought the stream was the source of Egypt's Nile River, which explorers to the north still had not been able to find.

They had no idea how many miles lay between the northern Transvaal and the Middle East, believing that they just had to trek a little farther north and they would be in the promised land.

In 2002, the town was renamed Modimolle, the name of a hill nearby that the early settlers believed might be a pyramid.

An unusual war tactic

During the frontier wars from 1779 to 1877 between the Xhosa and the advancing European settlers, the policy of the Xhosas was to kill or to torture the males in war, but to leave the women and girls unharmed.

Many stories tell of young colonial boys who dressed as girls, succeeded in fooling the enemy, and survived.

— *Graaff-Reinet, An illustrated historical guide*

PRESS SNIPPETS

1957

TRADITIONS

The visit of Confederate raider *Alabama* gave rise to the song *Daar kom die Alabama*

When the
U.S. CIVIL WAR
spread to Cape Town

Raphael Semmes

IN JULY 1863 the steamship *CSS Alabama* arrived in Saldanha Bay harbour, 120 km northwest of Cape Town.

This was no ordinary ship. It was the most infamous of the raiders that flew the Confederate flag during the U.S. civil war. Built in England in 1862 and commanded by Captain Raphael Semmes, a former U.S. Navy officer, it was a sailing ship, but also had a steam engine that it could use when necessary.

The *Alabama's* war-time mission was to raid federal merchant ships in the Atlantic, Indian and China seas carrying merchandise to or from the United States.

Its commanders would chase down the ships, rob them of their cargo and remove their sailors before burning the ships. The effort was aimed at restricting imports to the United States.

In a little more than a year, the *Alabama* captured 68 ships, causing millions of dollars in damage and became the "terror of the north" for the United States merchant fleet.

When the ship arrived unexpectedly in Saldanha Bay, many people from the area trekked to see it. Only a few farmers lived in Saldanha Bay at the time and most of them had never seen a steamer.

From Saldanha Bay, Semmes sent a message to Cape Colony Governor Wodehouse that he would like to visit Table Bay. Before he did, it became clear why the *Alabama* was in South African waters. The ship headed for *The Sea Bride*, a North American barque that had travelled south in the Atlantic Ocean toward the Cape in an attempt to avoid the Confederate raiders, only to encounter the worst of them off the Cape coast.

Crowds gather

As the two ships faced off in the sea off Table Bay, all business came to a standstill in Cape Town and crowds gathered on the shore from Green Point to Camps Bay to see the drama. They watched as the *Alabama* fired at *The Sea Bride*. It was a blank, but it

Business came to a stop

frightened the crew enough for them to submit. Soon the crowd saw the two ships enter Table Bay. There, the crowds besieged the *Alabama*. They were warmly welcomed by Semmes, who was greeted as a hero.

To avoid the *Alabama* raiding other ships, a British ship, the *H.M.S. Valorous,* was sent from Simon's Town and anchored alongside her.

The Cape Town Prize Court recognized *The Sea Bride* as legal capture. She was sold to a local shipping firm and used on the South African coast. You could say the Cape help notch a gain for the Confederate Navy.

Meanwhile the *Alabama* stocked up on coal in Simon's Town before setting off on a month's cruise. She had not gone far when a North American vessel arrived in search of her. Soon a game of hide-and-seek began in the Cape waters.

The *Alabama* succeeded in giving the North American ship the slip, returned to Cape Town to top up her coal supply, and slipped out under cover of darkness.

Ten months later, in July 1864, she was defeated by the North American ship the *Kearsage* in the waters off France, where she sank.

The drama was discussed for years in Cape Town. The song "Daar kom die *Alabama*" (There comes the *Alabama*) was written to commemorate the event and still lives on in Cape folk history.

Crew left behind

The story is told that some of the crew were inadvertently left behind in Saldanha Bay and settled there. Reports are that their graves,with an inscribed stone, may still be seen on an old farm in the district.

Kaapse Klopse origins

THE TRADITIONAL annual Kaapse Klopse Carnival, held at the New Year, is believed to have originated when sailors from the US Confederate ship *Alabama* paraded up Adderley Street in Cape Town, singing and dancing to guitars, while the ship was docked in Table Bay.

The local people thought that would be fun and adopted the custom. The Cape Town carnival troupes danced and sang their way up Adderley Street for more than a century.

Support for the *Alabama* theory comes from the names given to some of the troupes in the early days of the carnival: Mississippi Darkies, Kentucky Victorians, Cherry Pickers and Diamond Eyes.

Two other theories on the origin of the carnival:

*   It began as a celebration when the slaves were freed in Cape Town in 1832.

*   It began when a baker, C.J. Cole, provided his workers in 1894 with costumes and top hats to advertise his bread.

Perhaps it is a mixture of all three. You decide.

ORIGINAL TALE

𝔄 sobering encounter with an OSTRICH

EXTRACT FROM: *South African Sketches* by A.B. Ellis (1887)

PROBABLY, almost certainly, you will one day stop at a farm devoted to ostrich farming, a profitable business enough, but attended with risks peculiar to itself. Birds just hatched are worth £5, a half-grown one from £20 to £50, and as much as £100 is sometimes paid for brooding hens.

Should a wild ostrich happen to come along that way, he will carry off with him all the semi-domesticated birds, and the ostrich-farmer is ruined.

The birds are plucked before they are a year old. The operation is attended with some difficulty and danger. The kick of an ostrich will easily fracture a limb.

When several ostriches are to be plucked they are penned up closely together, so that there is no room for them to spread their wings or make a dart forward that appears to be the necessary preliminary of a kick, and the men can then go among them.

A fellow traveller

At some farms the half-grown ostriches run about round the house like domestic poultry. I remember this was the case at a farm, Du Plooi's, I think, near the Riet River.

We outspanned there one morning about ten, and arranged with the people to have some breakfast.

Among my fellow travellers was a young Englishman, who, ever since we had started from Cape Town, had been making conscientious endeavours to empty his flask of Cango brandy between every two halting-places. It was an internecine struggle, in which it seemed probable that the flask would be the victor. For the past day or two, the champion had been observed making wild clutches at imaginary flies in the air in front of his nose.

He looked suspiciously at the ostriches at this place, half doubting perhaps whether they were not mere creations of his brain, and they certainly did look ugly and ungainly creatures, for they had been plucked recently.

We went in to breakfast, which consisted of the invariable tough mutton-chop, fried in sheep-tail fat. I had a seat opposite the door, and my vis-a-vis was the young English man.

We had only been seated a few minutes when I observed an ostrich saunter in at the door. It came up behind the young man, peered quietly over his shoulder for an instant, and then, darting its head forward, snatched a mutton-chop out of his plate.

I shall never forget the look of horror which came into his face as this sudden apparition of a long, raw-looking, and snake-like neck, terminated in a pointed head with a very vicious eye, appeared over his shoulder. He uttered a loud shriek, dropped his knife and fork, and sprang to his feet. Everybody laughed as the ostrich retreated through the door, and our bacchanalian friend sat down again. But his appetite was gone and he was trembling all over.

Just before the wagon started, I was strolling round near the house, when I saw him, at the foot of a kopje, hurling stones violently at some object on the ground. Thinking he might be going to be ill, or that he was engaged in a frantic encounter with an imaginary snake, I approached softly, and saw that he was reducing his flask to the condition of powdered glass.

When he considered the fragments were sufficiently small, he crushed them under his heel, and returned to the wagon. Henceforward he drank no more.

His fright had produced good results. What a subject this would be for a temperance tract! It might be headed, "On the Verge of D. T.", or "Saved by an Ostrich," with a full-length portrait of the heaven-sent ostrich on the cover.

"THIS IS a regular German and Dutch house. The gentlemen keep the fire warm whilst the ladies perish in a cold hall or in their bedrooms. The gentlemen enjoy rich dinners whilst the ladies jump up and run about to serve them, the children alternately squall, are screamed at or get sweetmeats and are banished to the kitchen. I cannot get Baby near the fire in the drawing room whilst the gentlemen sit smoking with their hats on by it. Nevertheless, they are a kind hospitable household, only I think a little uncivilised...I am rather like a fish out of water, being accustomed to be petted and considered of most importance at home. It seems so strange to see others taking so little notice of their wives.

Your affectionate child, Emma Murray."

From: *Young Mrs. Murray goes to Bloemfontein, 1856–1860,* the story of a bride who spent the first years of her married life in Bloemfontein in its early days.

'Take a tickey with you'

BEFORE rands and cents replaced the British currency of pounds, shillings and pence in 1961, a popular South African coin was the tickey. It was worth three pennies. Four tickeys comprised a shilling.

The tickey was used for many years to operate public telephones and so was considered a useful coin to always have in one's pocket.

The word is believed to have originated from the word "tiga" which means three in Indonesian. Many slaves in Cape Town were brought to the Cape from that region.

Aloe there!

"Great quantities of the common aloe grow upon the plains that surround Muscle bay.* The inspissated** juice of this plant was once an article that afforded a considerable profit to those who were at the trouble of collecting and preparing it, but the price is now reduced so low, about threepence the pound, that it is no longer considered as an object worthy the attention of the inhabitants. Three pounds are as much as one person can collect and prepare in one day."

An Account of Travels Into the Interior of Southern Africa, in the Years 1797 and 1798 by Sir John Barrow.

* Today's Mossel Bay

** thickened or congealed

PEOPLES

FIRST CLASH

Set the tone for the future

The first encounter between European explorers and the indigenous people of southern Africa took place on November 7, 1497.

1497

Filled with misunderstanding and confusion, it set the tone for relationships between white and black in the subcontinent over the next 500 years.

The incident took place when Portuguese explorer Vasco Da Gama sailed south from Europe, reaching a curve in the African coast that he called St. Helena Bay. It still bears that name today.

Da Gama was the chief commander of 170 men on four ships *St. Gabriel, St. Raphael, Berrio*, and *Gonsalo Nunez*.

Da Gama landed to seek water and measure the altitude of the sun at noon to determine the latitude. The instrument for measuring vertical angles could not be used at sea as it needed to be mounted on a tripod and be steady.

He thereby became the first European to set foot on southern African soil in recorded history. While he was taking the measurements, the crew who accompanied him on shore saw two men, almost certainly Khoikhoi, who seemed to be gathering herbs. Because Da Gama wanted to learn something about the land, he ordered his men quietly to surround them. They did so and took one of the men captive.

Obviously, the Europeans could not understand what the terrified man was saying. Da Gama ordered two young men from one of his ships to talk with the Khoikhoi man. They offered him food and succeeded in making him less afraid.

Through sign language, Da Gama understood a village was

Vasco Da Gama

situated at the foot of a mountain that was fairly close. He presented the Khoikhoi man with trinkets, inviting him to return with others to receive more trinkets.

Pleasant meeting

The following day about 40 Khoikhoi appeared. They had as pleasant a meeting as possible when neither could understand the others' language.

When the Khoikhoi left, a soldier named Fernando Veloso went with them to find out more about the country.

Veloso did not like the meat that the Khoikhoi offered him and concluded that they were cannibals. He began to return to the ships and the Khoikhoi followed him. Fearing their intentions might be hostile, Veloso ran back, calling for help.

Seeing Veloso returning running over a hill, Da Gama left the ship to see whether he needed help. Believing their countryman to

Africa map in the 1665 Grooten Atlas

be in danger, other men also left the boats, attacking the approaching Khoikhoi. A skirmish took place in which Da Gama and three others were wounded with spears.

Once again, the Europeans ran to the safety of the ships, from which they fired their artillery on the "savages" on the shore.

Ten days later Da Gama set sail from St. Helena Bay.

They left behind them the first conflict between Europeans and the native inhabitants of South Africa, one which likely would have been avoided had the Europeans not regarded the Khoikhoi as warlike savages and even cannibals. It was only the first of many similar confrontations.

AFTER ROUNDING the Cape on his 1497 voyage from Portugal, explorer Vasco Da Gama passed a beautiful land that was a striking contrast with the sterile wastes on the western side of the continent. Because it was Christmas Day, they called it **Natal**, in memory of the day on which, they said, Christian men first saw it. Da Gama also named **St. Helena Bay** on the same voyage. Both names are still in use today, 520 years later.

WIVES WANTED

TWELVE YEARS after Jan van Riebeeck set up his trading station in 1652, the directors of the Dutch East India Company at the Cape tried to encourage young women from Holland to travel to the Cape under the care of clergymen and others with families. They were needed to provide wives for those men who were unmarried when discharged from the company's service at the Cape. The attempt failed.

In October 1685 Simon van der Stel, appointed commander of the colony in 1679, was told that 48 marriageable girls would be sent to the Cape from orphanages in Amsterdam and Rotterdam. The young women would need to travel under the care of a respectable elderly woman. They would also need to be properly cared for until they were married to honourable, sober and industrious burghers.

In the end only three young women from Rotterdam embarked on the voyage. They were followed by seven or eight the following year, Over the years small parties arrived consisting of only seven or eight at a time.

They were married to the wealthiest Cape burghers usually within a few weeks of landing.

THUMBQUOTE   66

What Cape Town looked like 400 years ago

EXTRACT FROM:

A Voyage to East-India

by the Rev. Edward Terry (1655)

In EUROPE, AFRICA, ASIA have I gone.

On arriving in Table Bay: June 12, 1615

"Our people, when they have come hither with very crazy bodies (from the disease scurvy), have often found here much good refreshing; for besides a most delectable brook of pure good water, arising hard by out of a mighty hill, (called from its form, the Table) close by which there is another hill, which ariseth exceeding high, like a pyramid, (and called by passengers, the Sugar Loaf) there are good store of cattle, called by the inhabitants, Boos; and sheep, which they call Baas, who bear a short, coarse, hairy wool, and I conceive are never shorn. These Boos and Baas as they call them, were formerly bought in great plenty, for small quantities of kettle brass, and iron hoops taken off our empty casks.

This remotest part of Africa is very mountainous, over-run with wild beasts, as lions, tigers, wolves, and many other beasts of prey, which in the silent night discover themselves by their noise and roaring; to the teeth and jaws of which cruel beasts, the natives here expose their old people, if death prevent it not, when once they grow very old and troublesome, laying them in some open place, in the dark night…One miserable poor old wretch was thus exposed when we were there; who by his pitiful cries was discovered by our court of guard, there on shore, and not far off from him, and by them relieved and delivered for that present time out of the jaws of death."

Four decades ago...

SOUTHERN AFRICA

was ahead of

New York

Jutten Island

S outhern Africa had its own Coney Island before New York named its iconic island, which was later joined to the mainland and became known for its funfair attractions and beach.

Here s what happened: On April 3, 1605 the 240-ton English ship Tiger sailed past a little island off Saldanha four months after setting sail from Cowes an English seaport town on the Isle of Wight on its way to the Indies.

The ship's general, Sir Edward Michelburne, and seven men rowed in a skiff to the island.

"While we were on shore they in the ship had a storm," the general

recorded in the ship's journal, "which drove them out of sight of the island; and we were two days and two nights before we could recover our ship.

"Upon the said island is abundance of great conies and seals, whereupon we called it Coney Island." A coney is a rabbit, but the animals on the island were probably dassies, also known as rock rabbits or coneys.

The name of the New York attraction dates back to 1664, almost 60 years after the South African island first bore the name.

The Tiger's journal said the island was five or six leagues (about 15 to 18 sea miles or 25 km) from Saldanha. It was likely today's Jutten Island.

A dassie or rock rabbit

False signal?

IN JULY 1620 a fleet of four British ships under Andrew Shillinge put into Table Bay. Two days later he and Humphrey Fitzherbert, who arrived in an English fleet a few days later, decided that no better place would be found and proclaimed English sovereignty over the country. They drew up a formal document to that effect addressed to the king. They said it was better that they take possession rather than the Dutch, or any other nation.

"The whale fishery persuades us that it would be profitable to defray part of the charge," they told the king. "The fruitfulness of the soil, together with the temper of the air, assures us that the Blacks, with the time, will come in, for their safety and of necessity. Time will no doubt make them your servants, and by serving you they will become hereafter (we hope) the servants of God."

They hoisted a flag on a hill they called King James Mount, which later was called Lion's Rump and today is known as Signal Hill. They sailed off and never took actual possession of the country.

LOST TREASURE

R3 million
LOST
in the dunes

T he mail was considerably slower 110 years ago. Letters sent by sea took up to six weeks to reach their addressees. Even mail delivered by wagon across land could take weeks.

Often currency or precious metals, such as gold or silver, were sent by mail.

Some never reached their intended recipients, leading to speculation on how many fortunes are waiting to be found in undelivered mail lying in desolate parts of Southern Africa.

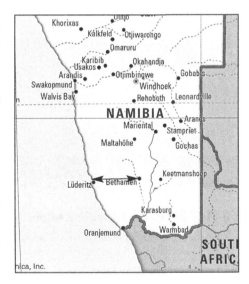

Given up for lost

Here's a story of one such treasure.

On January 12, 1905 Trooper Fiebecke and an official named Rogge left Luderitz, in today's Namibia, on horseback carrying 20,000 German marks (about £1,000 in those days and R3 million today). They were headed for a garrison at Bethanien, about 230 km away, much of it over desert.

100 German marks (1900)

The men became lost in the sand dunes.

A search was launched to find them, but their tracks had been blown away. They were given up for lost.

Six years later a Khoikhoi man found Fiebecke's belt and bayonet. He handed them to the police. A new search was launched, but it was unsuccessful.

In 1912 a police patrol stumbled across Rogge's body. His notebook contained a farewell message to his mother and sister in Germany. He said the horses had run away and he was about to shoot himself to avoid dying of thirst.

Letters and the 20,000 German marks were in a bag alongside Rogge's body. The letters and the money were delivered intact—seven years after they were mailed.

HOME REMEDIES

TO STOP BLEEDING FROM THE NOSE: A teaspoonful of cream of tartar in a tumbler of water, taken, will almost immediately stop the bleeding.

FOR BRUISES OR SPRAINS: Bathe with hot water as soon as it can possibly be procured, and as hot as can be borne. Go on for an hour or more.

From *Hilda's Where is it?* (1891)

PEOPLE

WHEN

George Bernard Shaw

S U R F E D

at Muizenberg

YES, IT'S TRUE. The 75-year-old man you see surfing at Muizenberg IS George Bernard Shaw. Of course you know who he was. He was the author, among other works, of Pygmalion, which later was adapted to become the classic musical My Fair Lady.

Shaw visited Cape Town in 1932. He stayed at a hotel in Muizenberg, thought he would try surfing for the first time in his life, and pretty soon he was hooked.

He had booked to stay for two weeks. Instead he stayed for a month. And he had as much fun as he had ever had in his life. Here he is showing off his board. Okay, okay. So today we call it a boogie board. You still go surfing with it, wise guy.

Shaw went on the next year to visit America for the first time in his life. We like to think he preferred surfing at Muizenberg.

ANOTHER famous author, **Agatha Christie,** surfed at Muizenberg during a world trip in January 1922. She fell in love with surfing and was among the first people to surf standing up.

DISASTERS

South Africa's

W⊙RST
MINE
DISASTER

Miners in the rescue team drink coffee after two gruelling hours underground. They are carrying respirators and oxygen cylinders. The miner on the left is holding a cage with a canary to detect methane gas. *(Rand Daily Mail)*

O n January 21, 1960, 425 men were trapped in the north shaft of Coalbrook mine in the Orange Free State. The men were trapped when two large sections of the mine collapsed. They were suffocated by methane gas and then were crushed by falling rocks.

G.S. van der Merwe, who was underground when the mine collapsed told *The Star* newspaper how he was able to escape.

"At about 7:20 p.m. we tested for gas and realised that something was wrong. The meter indicated that the gas in the mine was rising rapidly. The mine captain told us to get out, but warned us not to run. I started walking. The next moment there was a tremendous blast of wind through the tunnel.

"I grabbed a pole and hung on with all my strength. When everything settled down again I found myself alone. Around me was chaos. My eyes and mouth were full of sand and I could hardly see Suddenly I saw a light a few yards ahead of me. It was Basie Schankan. We left the mine together. On the surface we heard that the others were also safe."

Most of the men who fled after the first rockfall were trapped by the second, however. A giant drill was used to try to reach the men After being used daily for five days, it reached a depth of only 175 feet; the men were trapped at 515 feet and the drill was never able to reach them. No signs of life were detected by a microphone lowered down.

After 11 days, on February 5, all attempts at rescue were called off. All 425 had died.

PEOPLE

How Harry Bolus found a new purpose in life

B ritish-born Harry Bolus read every book on botany before he was 12. In 1849—attracted by the rich diversity of plant life he had heard existed in South Africa—he emigrated at the age of 15. Before too long he became a leading banker in Graaff-Reinet and later moved to Grahamstown where he married Sophia Kensit.

Bolus was devastated when their six-year-old son died from diphtheria in spite of his use of homeopathic medicine to save him.

Even those who knew Bolus well were appalled at the effect the loss of his son had on him. He could not settle down to work. He could not sleep. He could not read. He slumped into a deep depression.

A good friend, Francis Guthrie, told him: "You should find a hobby to which you can dedicate yourself to take your mind off your loss. What are you interested in?" Bolus thought it could be botany. "Go ahead devote yourself to it now," Guthrie responded. From that day, Bolus found a new purpose in life.

When his brother Walter left England to set up a firm in Cape Town, he invited Harry to join him. Harry was hesitant until he heard of the wealth of flora on the slopes of Table Mountain. He realised he could pursue his hobby more fully in Cape Town.

Through the 1870s and 1880s he collected the best examples of flora from the Cape Peninsula. He wrote many scientific publications including, with Professor Guthrie, *Flora Capensis*, a great botanical work of the time. He became wealthy working in investment banking at the same time. He died in 1911, leaving nearly £27,000 to the upkeep of the herbarium attached to the University of Cape Town, which still bears his

PARTING SHOTS

Whatever it takes...

A widow living in Cape Town in 1754 refused to allow her two children to attend a church-run school.

Church elders reminded her of her duty. The church minister reprimanded her. She still kept the children at home.

Her refusal was taken a step higher. The Council of Policy admonished her, telling her not to raise her children as heathens. She remained obstinate.

"I have the right to have my children educated or not, as I please," she told them.

Finally the issue was brought before Governor Ryk Tulbagh. He ordered her to take her children to the church school so that they could be instructed in the Christian way.

If she did not comply, she was told, she would be flogged.

Wisely, she finally submitted.

"Now I never said I wouldn't eat it, honey. I just asked what it was."

This 1970 cartoon is a reminder of the days in which every wife was expected to cook an evening meal for her husband when he returned home from work.

The Star, Sept. 17, 1970

PARTING SHOTS

How dagga* was smoked

❝The use of tobacco is universal, that plant being indigenous; and they (the Fingoes) are also much addicted to smoking the wild hemp called 'dacca'* which they cultivate for the purpose. The smaller leaves of this plant are dried in the sun, and being ground fine, the fumes are inhaled through a pipe, exciting the nervous system frightfully, and more especially affecting the lungs in a most violent manner, the smoker being subjected to violent paroxysms of spasmodic coughing, which eventually leaves him in a stupid dreamy state, accompanied by utter mental and bodily prostration.

The Muntatees and other tribes, when provided with pipes, have an ingenious method of smoking the 'dacca' out of the ground, moistening the earth and stamping it with their naked feet into a stiff clay, they form the stem of the pipe by passing a long curved twig through the soil in a semi-circular direction. The hole is made by enlarging one end where it reaches the surface with the finger; into this they put the lighted 'dacca' and apply their mouths to the other end, each inspiration being accompanied by a draught of water.❞

Cape Town was home to an elite roller skating rink in 1890. This picture is from a newspaper advertisement at the time.

* marijuana

—*Camp Life and Sport in South Africa* by T.J. Lucas (published 1878)

In the 1850s, many Filipinos arrived in Cape Town to work in the fishing industry, particularly around Kalk Bay. Filipino family names can still be found in Kalk Bay and Filipino words still occur in the local dialect.

QUICK QUIZ

All the answers are to be found in this book.

1. Which precious metal was involved in a scam played on Cape Governor Simon van der Stel?
   a. Silver
   b. Gold
   c. Platinum

2. Who did a Khoikhoi man named Klaas Velletjes meet in London in the 1880s?
   a. Prime Minister William Gladstone
   b. King James
   c. Queen Victoria

3. What was the hot new car advertised in 1957?
   a. Oldsmobile Cutlass
   b. Hudson Custom Rambler
   c. Volkswagen Rabbit

4. In which South African bay did the *CSS Alabama* first arrive?
   a. Table Bay
   b. Saldanha Bay
   c. Simon's Bay

5. What name did the Voortrekkers give to Modimolle?
   a. Nylstroom
   b. Potgietersrust
   c. Randfontein

ANSWERS: Page 64

CROSSWORD PUZZLE

All the answers are in this book.
Answers to puzzle: Page 64

ACROSS

5. A reverend story gatherer
10. An ostrich took it
11. Doctor for Port of London
12. Modimolle thought to be this
15. Name of prevailing wind
16. River flooded in 1875
18. Picture Palace
20. He wrote about an ostrich
21. It means 'people of'
24. Nickname of a coin
25. Khoikhoi originated here
26. Oil used in cooking
27. Origin of coin's name
28. Hudson dealer
29. Da Gama's first name

DOWN

1. Smallpox medical officer
2. Diamond finder Campbell
3. Gordon's ___
4. Where Velletjes was from
6. Dish that must simmer
7. Some Kalk Bay word origins
8. 1767 virus came on this ship
9. A Cape Town mayor
13. It hit Cape Town in 1962
14. Another name for a dassie
17. Virus that causes smallpox
19. It's 230 km from Luderitz
22. Semmes' first name
23. He met Queen Victoria
24. Valley or mountain name

ANSWERS TO PUZZLES

Answers to Past Pictures on Page 26:

1: Queens Hotel, Kimberley, 1880s
2: Jubilee Square, Simon's Town, 1890s
3: The Exchange, Cape Town, 1832

Answers to Quick Quiz on Page 62:

1a; 2c; 3b; 4b; 5a

Answer to crossword puzzle on Page 63:

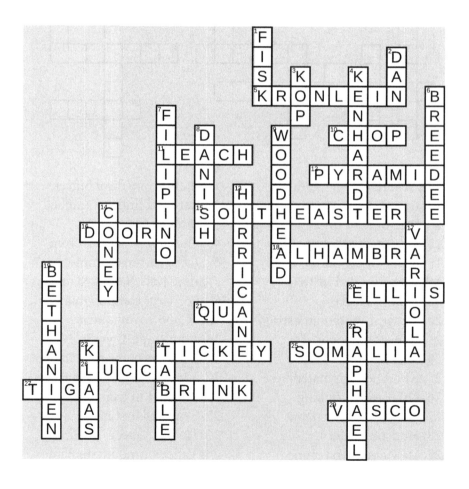

Made in the USA
Middletown, DE
17 November 2022